the
celsius
thermometer
is

the celsius thermometer is

By Jerolyn Ann Nentl

Library of Congress Catalog Card Number: 76-24205. International Standard Book Number: 0-913940-48-8.

Design - Doris Woods and Randal M. Heise

Special Thanks to:

Dr. Mary Kahrs - Professor of Education at Mankato State University, Mankato, Minnesota

Mr. David L. Dye - Mathematics Consultant, St. Paul, Minnesota

PHOTO CREDITS

Mark Ahlstrom, Media House

R.M. Heise - Art Director

the celsius thermometer is

Have you ever used a thermometer at home or at school? Perhaps you wanted to see how hot a day it was or if it was cold enough to wear a sweater. Or maybe your parents or the school nurse thought you had a fever and they used a thermometer to find out your body temperature.

In the metric system the unit for measuring temperature is the DEGREE CELSIUS. You will always see Celsius spelled with a capital letter because it is really the last name of the man who invented the Celsius thermometer. He was Anders Celsius and he lived in Sweden about 200 years ago.

Anders Celsius was an astronomer. His science was that of the sun and the moon, the stars and the other planets. As a scientist he often used a thermometer.

ANDERS CELSIUS

But Celsius thought the thermometers being used were too complicated. So in 1742 he invented one he thought was easier to use.

Like other thermometers, it had a glass tube that held mercury. Mercury is a liquid chemical that is very sensitive to heat and cold. It expands or gets bigger when it is heated, and it contracts or gets smaller when it is cooled. The hotter the mercury gets the higher it rises in the glass tube. As it gets colder, the mercury falls lower and lower down the tube.

We can study the rise and fall of temperatures by watching the mercury rise and fall in a thermometer.

Celsius decided to divide his thermometer into 100 units or grades. He called it a centigrade thermometer. Remember, the prefix "centi" means 1/100.

When measuring temperature you write °C after the number.

°C means DEGREE CELSIUS.

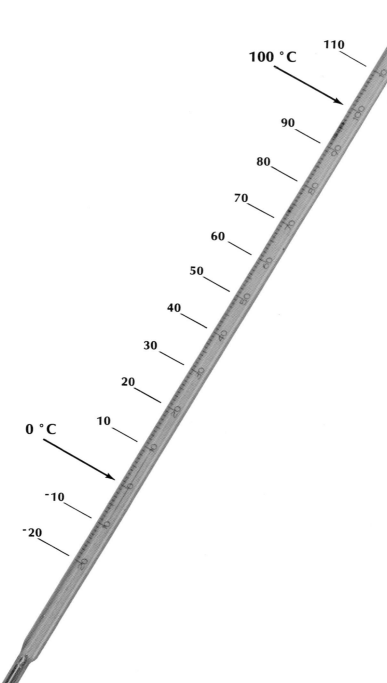

110

100 °C

90

80

70

60

50

40

30

20

10

0 °C

-10

-20

13

To find starting and ending points on his thermometer, Celsius boiled some water. He put the glass tube filled with mercury into the boiling water and watched to see how high the mercury rose in the tube. At its highest point he marked a line and wrote 100.

After he let the glass tube cool he put ice in a container and put the tube into the ice. He marked a line at the point where the mercury came in the tube and wrote 0. These starting and ending points are called REFERENCE POINTS.

Then Celsius divided the space on the tube between the two reference points into 100 equal units and called each unit a DEGREE, just as other scientists had called the units on their thermometers. Each degree is 1/100 of the total distance between the point at which water freezes and the point at which water boils.

With the Celsius thermometer water freezes at 0 °C and boils at 100 °C.

Most thermometers have extra degrees marked below 0 °C, and some also have extra degrees marked above 100 °C, so that temperatures colder than freezing water, and hotter than boiling water can also be measured.

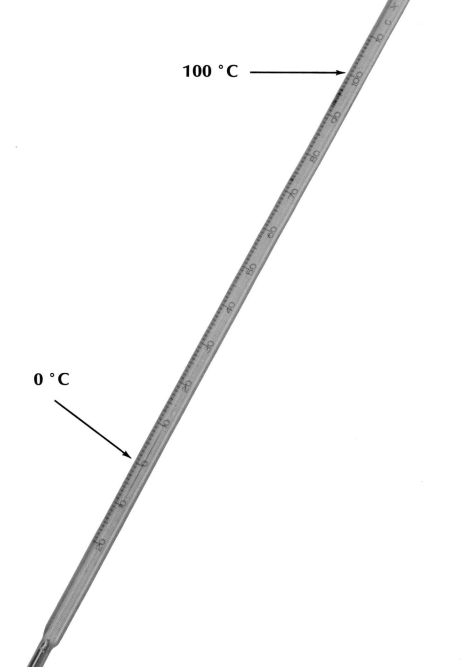

100 °C

0 °C

Let's look at some temperatures and see what they mean.

Most people think a comfortable temperature for a room in a house, school, or office building is about 20 °C.

If the temperature outside is 20 °C, or anywhere between 15 °C and 25 °C, it is a very comfortable day. If it gets about 25 °C, it is a very hot day and the sun is probably shining very brightly. A very hot day would be 40 °C.

It can get to be 45 °C or 50 °C in the Sahara desert.

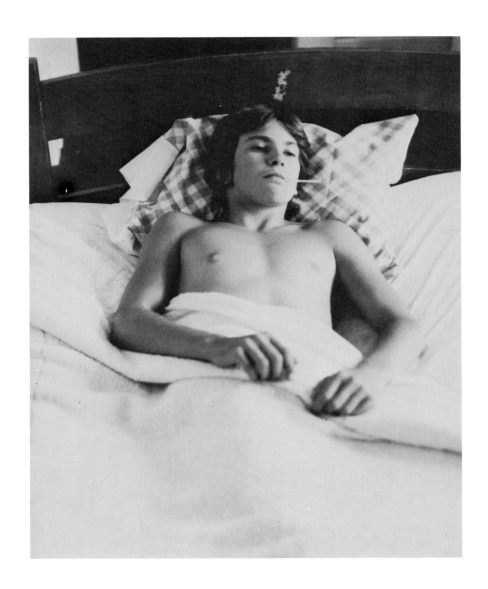

A person's normal body temperature is 37 °C. If it gets to be above 40 °C, it is time to call the doctor.

The fish will like it if you keep the water in your aquarium at about 24 °C. Goldfish like cooler temperatures.

The formula in a baby's bottle is about the same as your body temperature of 37 °C.

If it is 18 °C or lower, it is a cool day. This is spring or autumn weather, and you will probably wear a sweater or light jacket. When it gets very cold, the temperature may drop 10° below the zero mark on the Celsius thermometer. We read this "10 degrees Celsius below zero," or "10 degrees below zero Celsius," and we write it like this: ⁻10 °C.

When it gets ⁻5 °C, the lakes in some northern states freeze. Almost all lakes and rivers would be frozen by -15 °C.

To bake a cake the oven must be set somewhere between 154 °C and 177 °C.

The temperature in your refrigerator should be between 5 °C and 10 °C.

The Celsius thermometer was recognized as part of the metric system in 1927. It is the thermometer used by people in their everyday lives when they change to the metric system.

The other method of measuring temperature in the metric system is the Kelvin thermometer. This is the thermometer used by scientists.

The Kelvin thermometer uses a centigrade scale like the Celsius thermometer, but the units are called DEGREES KELVIN instead of degrees Celsius.

Kelvin did not like the idea of having "below zero" temperatures. He said that the temperature of something could be zero only when all the heat is taken from it.

LORD KELVIN

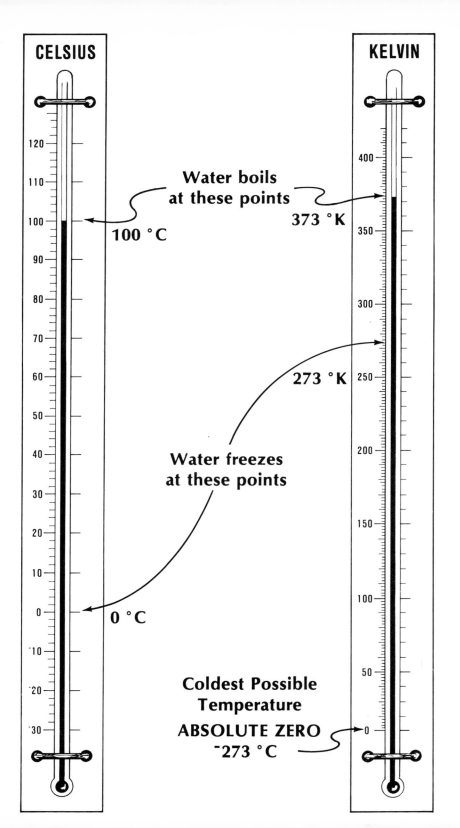

CELSIUS

KELVIN

Water boils
at these points

100 °C

373 °K

273 °K

Water freezes
at these points

0 °C

Coldest Possible
Temperature
ABSOLUTE ZERO
⁻273 °C

Scientists now believe that the coldest temperature possible is ⁻273 °C. Kelvin took this temperature and called it ABSOLUTE ZERO. He used it for the zero point of his scale, just as Celsius had taken the temperature at which water freezes as the zero point of the scale for his thermometer.

On the Kelvin thermometer water freezes at 273 °K and boils at 373 °K. Do you see how you get these numbers?

You will know which thermometer is being used in a metric system temperature reading by looking to see which kind of degree is used.

C means Celsius

K means Kelvin

Remember, the CELSIUS thermometer is used for every day measures of temperature when using the Metric System.

Now that you know about

the celsius thermometer

you should meet the rest of the Metric family.

the metric system is

the liter is

the gram is

the meter is

from